# WRITE ABOUT IT

## Beginning Writers

by Imogene Forte

Incentive Publications, Inc.   Nashville, Tennessee

Thank You

to Mary Catherine Mahoney, editor
to Becky Cutler, cover designer
to Mary Hamilton, artist

ISBN # 0-86530-044-5

# This Book Belongs to

_____

# WRITE ABOUT IT . . .

I can write...

- numbers
- letters
- words
- sentences
- rhymes
- paragraphs
- conversations
- notes
- stories

. . . and more!

*Write About It—Beginning Writers* is made up of fun-filled activities to provide writing growth for boys and girls. Each page has been carefully designed to introduce and reinforce one or more writing skills. Simple directions, fanciful themes, and the use of a controlled vocabulary allow purposeful early writing.

*Write About It—Beginning Writers* is based on the premise that children learn to read and write more quickly when they are able to associate learning activities with personal experiences. The purpose of this book is to help children speak, listen, read, and write naturally about their own experiences. This language experience approach diminishes threat and helps young children encounter the joy of expressing themselves through writing.

In addition to the focus on specific writing skills, each activity provides additional readiness development. The variety of drawing, coloring, tracing, cut-and-paste, dot-to-dot, visual discrimination, and figure ground activities afford a high interest level as well as skills reinforcement. They may be used in an individual or group setting.

Imogene Forte

# HOW TO USE THIS BOOK: A GUIDE FOR PARENTS AND TEACHERS

The *Write About It—Beginning Writers* pages allow young children to create as they write. The worksheets are more than fill-in-the-blank activities: for each blank, more than one word choice is given. Thus each child's resulting story will truly be his or her own.

This guide and the table of contents which follows offer a step-by-step explanation of how *Write About It—Beginning Writers* can be used most successfully.

*The first step* in preparing to use this book is to construct the word card envelope, which can be found on the last page of the book. The child cuts out the envelope, folds along the dotted lines, and pastes or tapes where indicated, leaving the flap unpasted. The child may then personalize the envelope as desired. (If the book is to be used by an individual child, the envelope may be pasted on the inside back cover; in a classroom, children or the teacher may keep the envelopes available for use.)

*The second step* is to prepare the word cards as they are needed. There are two types of word cards: those with corresponding pictures, and those with a word for the child to trace.

I. *Word cards with pictures.* To prepare these cards, the child colors and cuts out the picture cards. With help, the child matches each picture or numeral with its proper word card to reinforce the word, then pastes it in place.

II. *Word cards with traceable words.* These cards are completed by the child's tracing the word from left to right, thus providing first-hand experience with the word.

*Step three* is to go over the finished word cards carefully and patiently until the child is familiar with them. Examples given should include singular forms of verbs and plural forms of nouns, e.g., look/looks; see/sees; girl/girls; bird/birds. A blank word card page is included so the parent or teacher can make additional cards to include other words which are known to the child.

*Now it is time* to begin the writing activities themselves. The table of contents indicates which specific word cards should be provided. To present an activity page, the proper word cards are selected, and the child is told to put those word cards on the desk or table. It is important for the child to know that there are more word cards than necessary, and that he or she may make up his or her own story by choosing which word cards to use. The child should understand and be reminded that any words printed in the title or directions are also available for use.

When the *Write About It—Beginning Writers* activities are completed in the order presented, the young child progresses through a logical sequence by first writing letters and numerals, then selecting from limited words, and finally writing his or her own sentences, paragraphs, and creative stories. The completion certificate (see page 38) should be filled in and presented to the new writer. It may be used on its own or as the cover of a booklet which the child can make by putting all the completed activities in order.

# TABLE OF CONTENTS

# I CAN WRITE
# LOWERCASE LETTERS

a  b  c  d  e  f

g  h  i  j  k  l  m

n  o  p  q  r  s

t  u  v  w  x  y

z

# I CAN WRITE
# CAPITAL LETTERS

A B C D E

F G H I J

K L M N O

O P Q R

S T U V

W X Y Z

# THE LETTER TRAIN

## Write the missing capital letters.

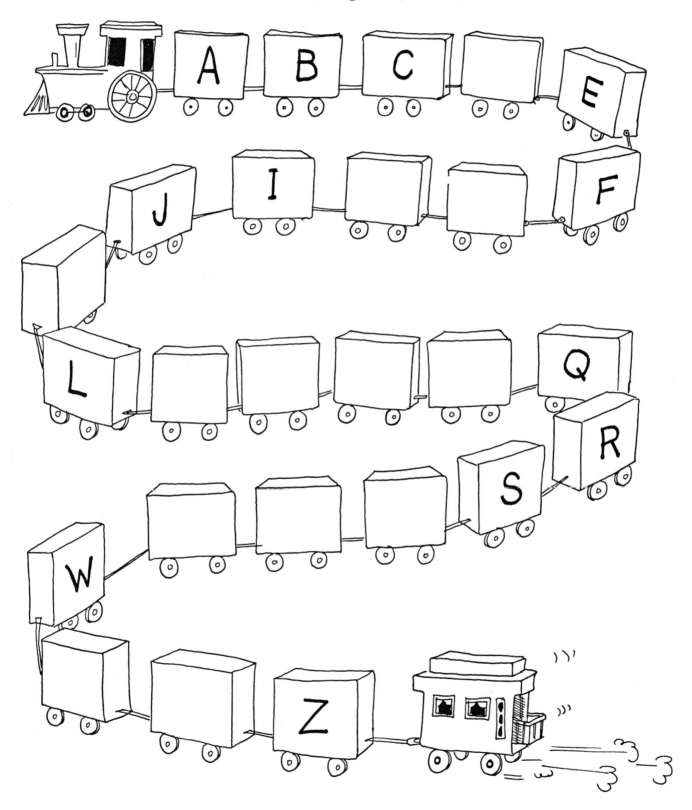

# THE NUMBER WORM

Write the missing numbers.

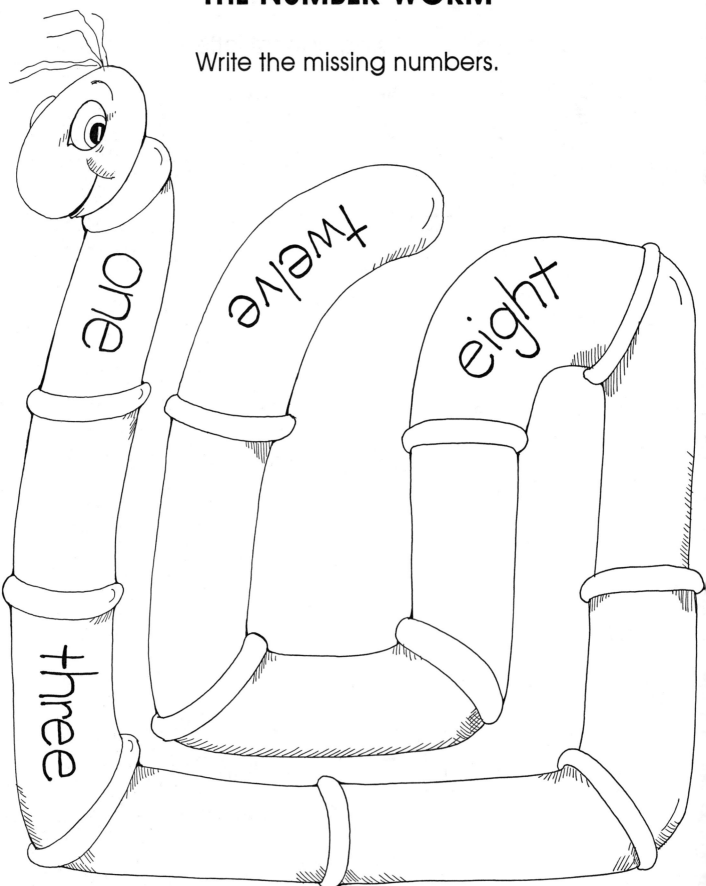

# NUMERALS

I can write my numerals from 1 to _____ .

# SCHOOL DAYS

Draw faces to show how the children feel about school.

SCHOOL BUS

The children _____ school.

They are _____.

# TEACHER, TEACHER

Write about your teacher.

I _____ my

teacher _____

of the time .

# WRITE ABOUT THE DOGS

One dog is _____.

One dog is _____.

They like _____.

# WRITE ABOUT THE CAT

The _____ is _____.

He likes to _____

_____

# WRITE A RHYME

I look and look

for a good

The little

sleeps in a hat.

# JANE'S DREAM

Draw Jane's dream.

Jane is dreaming
about

# THE CAKE

Look ! Look !

The _____ made

a _____ cake !

The cake looks

_____ .

# BEN'S BIRTHDAY

### Draw Ben's wish.

Ben is _____.

He is wishing

for _____.

# WORD BAG

Fill this bag with words you like to write.

# A COAT FOR THE RABBIT

Trace and color the rabbit's coat.
Write three words that tell how the rabbit looks.

# HOW IS THE WEATHER?

Write two words that tell about each picture.
Color the pictures.

# WRITE A TITLE FOR THE STORY

The dog is fast.

The duck is last.

# WHAT WILL HAPPEN NEXT?

Look at the _____

_____

_____

# BIRDS OF A FEATHER

## Color the two birds that match.
## Write about the other bird.

# UP, UP, AND AWAY

Color the balloons.
Write about the balloons.

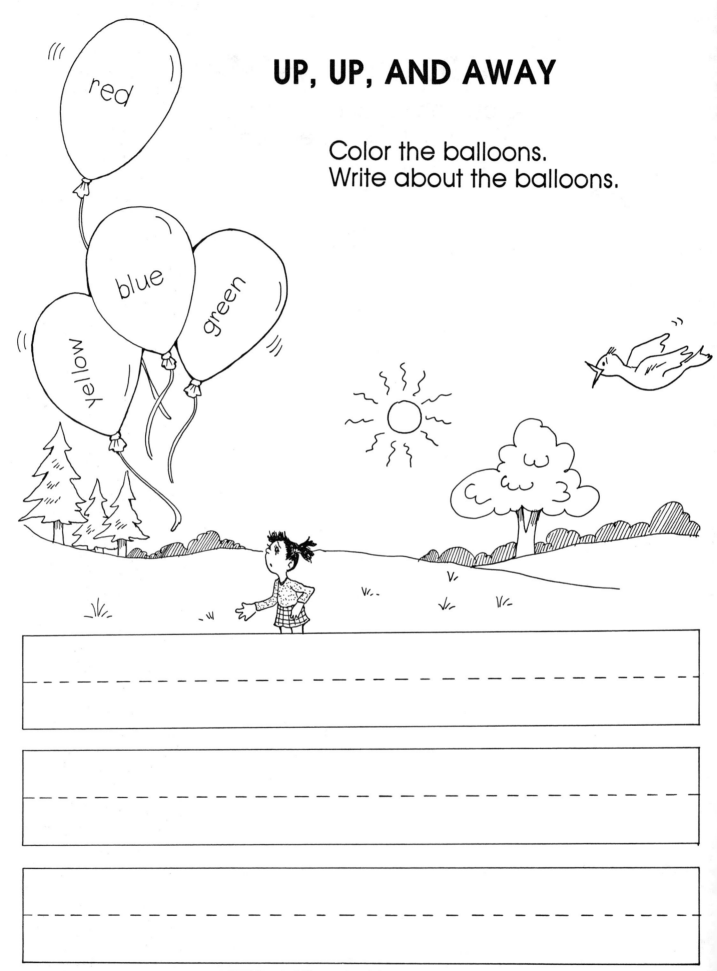

red

blue

green

yellow

# I SEE RED

## Color three things red.
## Write about the red things.

# A FUNNY FACE

Draw a funny face on the pumpkin.
Color it orange and black.
Write about it.

# WRITE WHAT THEY SAY

Write what the boy says.
Write what the teacher says.

# TWO DUCKS

Draw two ducks.
Write about the ducks.

# DOT-TO-DOT
Draw dot-to-dot.
Write about the snowman.

# THREE HIDDEN HOUSES

Find three hidden houses.
Write about the one you would like to live in.

# NOTE FOR A FRIEND

Write a note to a friend.
Address the note and send it.

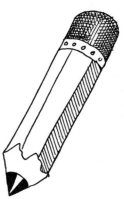

cut

- - - - - - - - - - - - - - - - - - - - - - - - - fold - - - - - - - - - - - - - - - - - - - - - - - - -

stamp

_____

_____

_____

# PICTURE FOR A FRIEND

Draw a picture for a friend.
Write about it.
Send it to your friend.

cut

------- fold -------------------

# DRAW A DRIVER FOR THE CAR

Write about the driver.

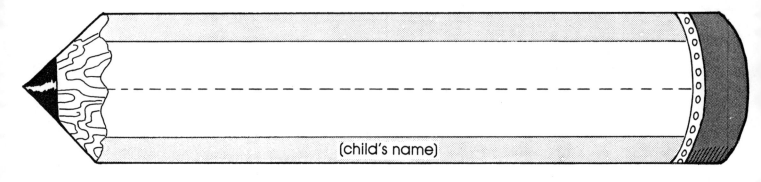

(child's name)

can write numbers, numerals, letters, words, sentences, paragraphs, and stories.

I can WRITE ABOUT IT!

_____
signed

_____
date

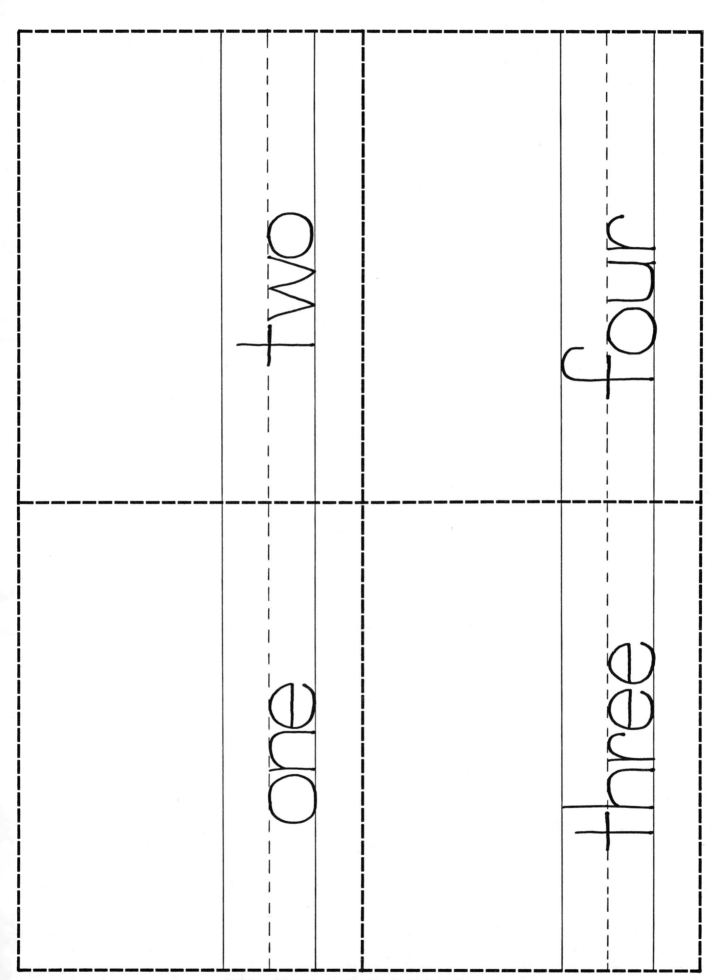

one

two

three

four

five

six

seven

eight

ten

nine

twelve

eleven

yellow

green

red

blue

black

duck

orange

rabbit

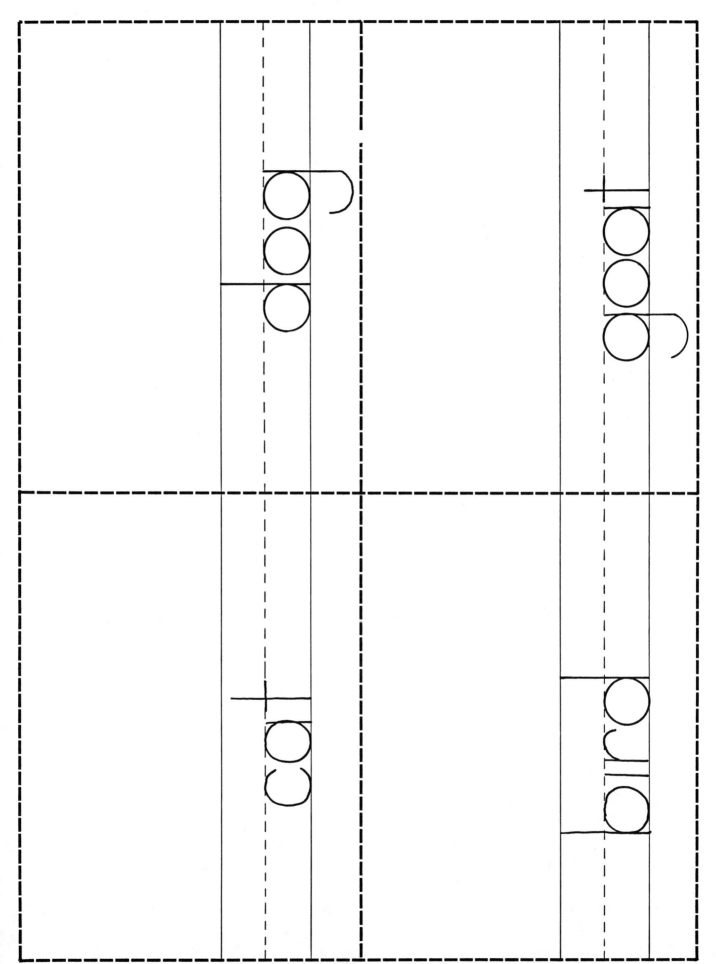

dog

cat

goat

bird

toot

sos

toys

happy

candy

cook

cake

apple

book

teacher

girl

boy

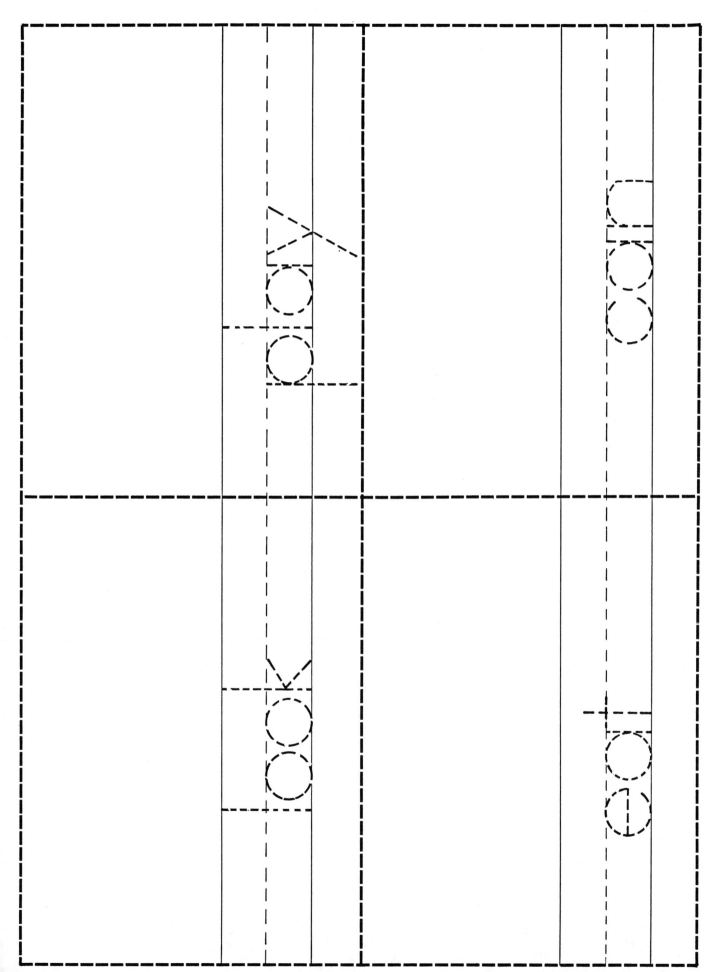

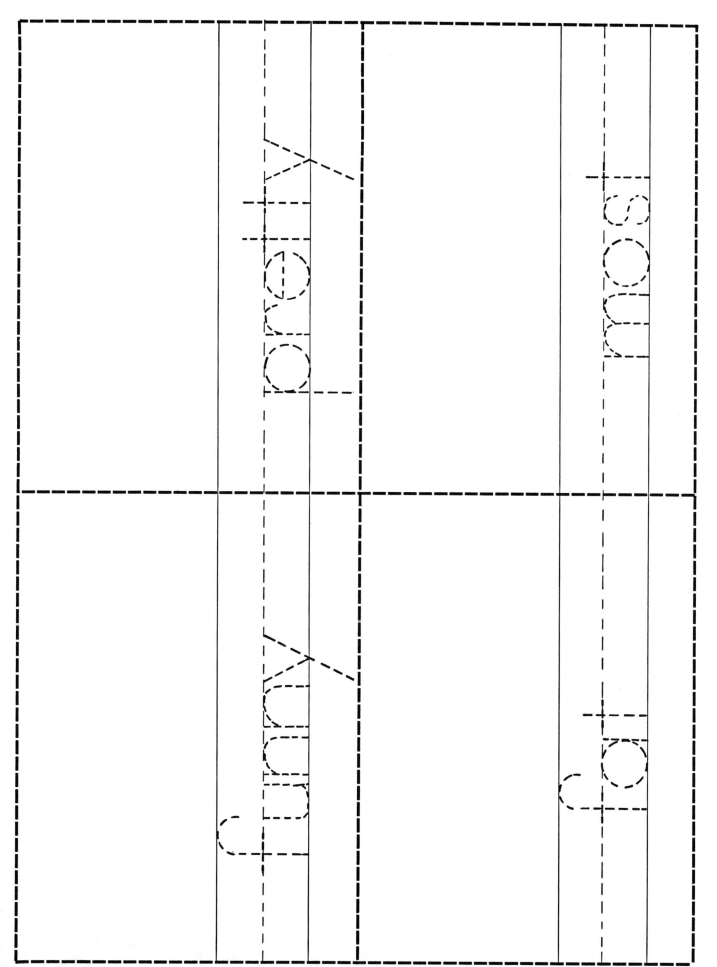

eye

room

love

run

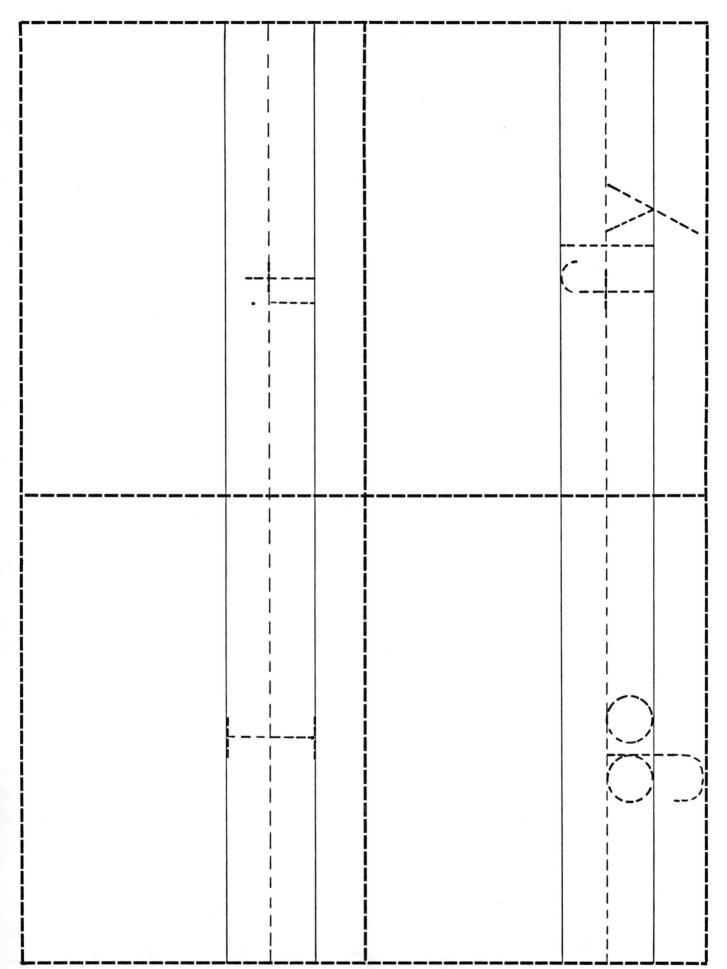

4

5

6

1

2

3

10

11

12

7

8

9

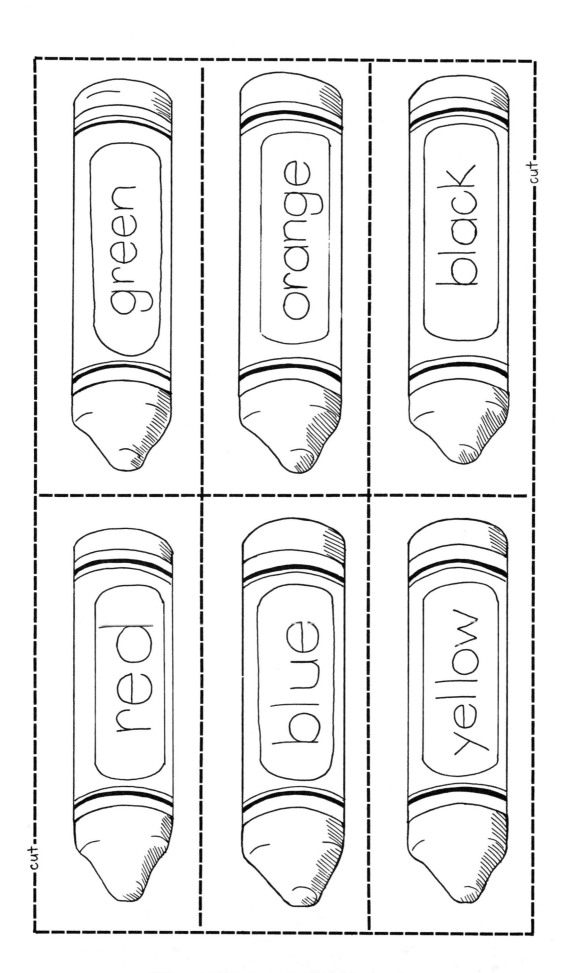

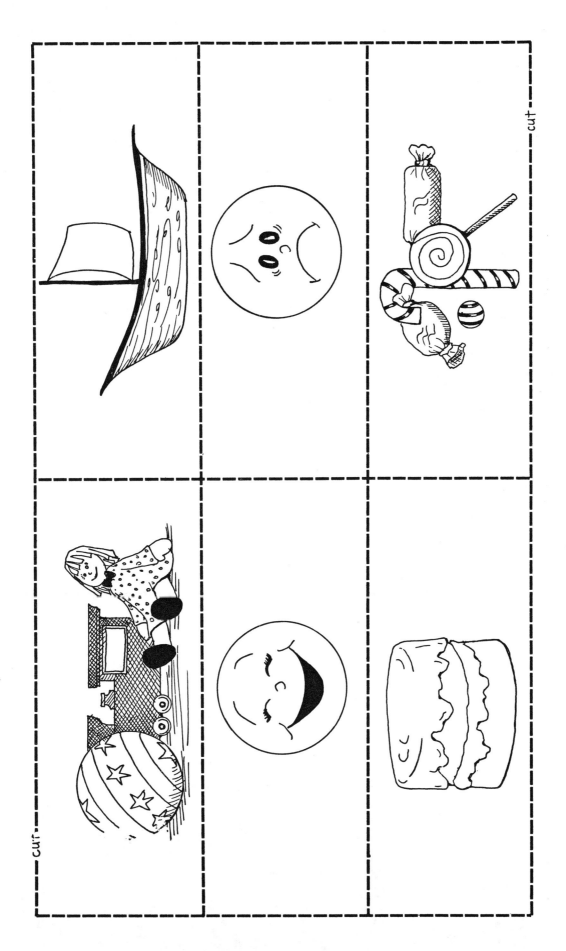

C

cut

cut

- - - - - - - - - - - - - - - fold - - - - - - - - - - - - - - -

fold

fold

B

- - - - - - - - - - - - - fold - - - - - - - - - - - - -

cut

cut

## <u>Instructions for Making the Word Card Envelope</u>

1. Cut along all solid lines.
2. Fold lower flap (A) to inside along dotted line.
3. Fold outer flaps (B) toward center along dotted lines and tape or paste securely.
4. Insert word cards in envelope and fold upper flap (C) down for storage (a bit of tape may be used to "seal" the envelope).

A

_____'s

**word cards**